'Look out of the window,' said Kevin.
Ben looked.
He saw a snake in the grass.

The boys ran outside, and picked up the snake. He was heavy.

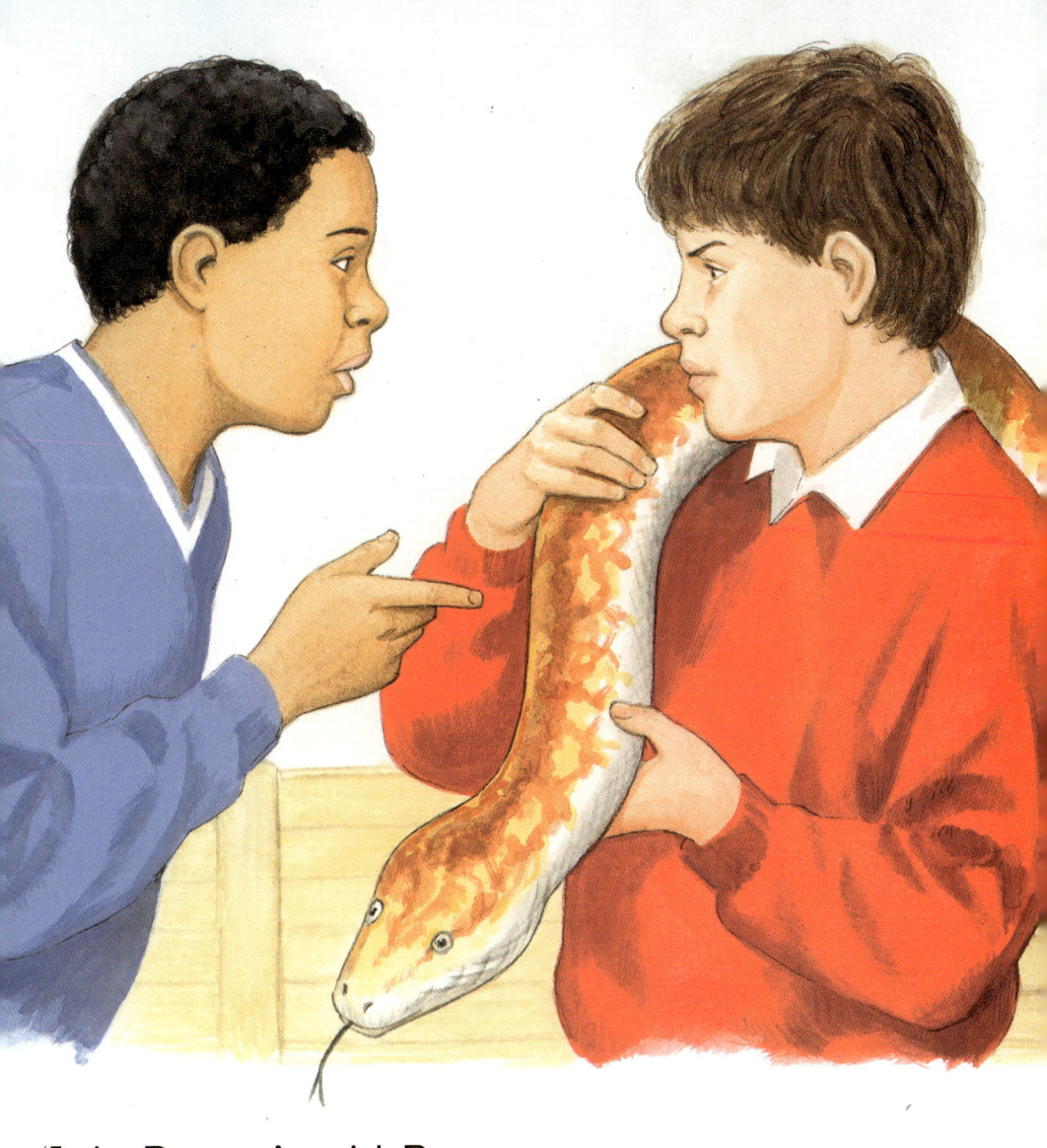

'It is Bruce,' said Ben.
'We can take him to Mr Keeping.'
But Kevin wanted to play with the snake.
'We can take him later,' he said.

The boys played with Bruce all day.
Later, Ben had to go home.

Mr Keeping looked for Bruce all over.
He asked Ben about the snake.
Ben said, 'Kevin has him.'

They went to see Kevin.
'Do you have my snake?' asked Mr Keeping.
'No,' said Kevin.
'Yes, you do!' said Ben.
'The snake is in the shed.'

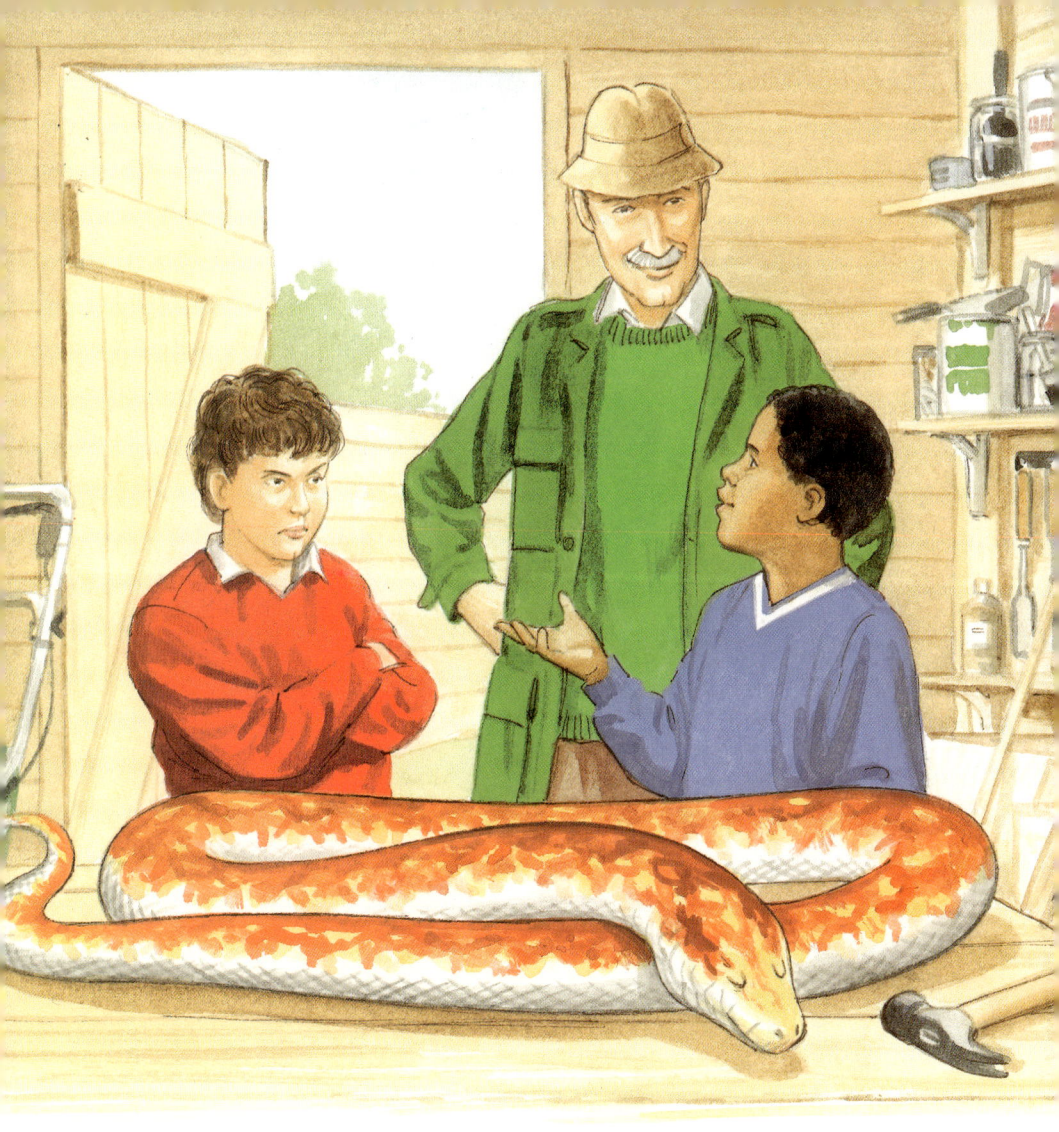

They opened the shed door.
There was Bruce.
Bruce looked happy, but Kevin looked cross.
He wanted to keep the snake.

Mr Keeping smiled.
'You boys can look after Bruce when I am away,' he said.
'Yes!' they shouted.